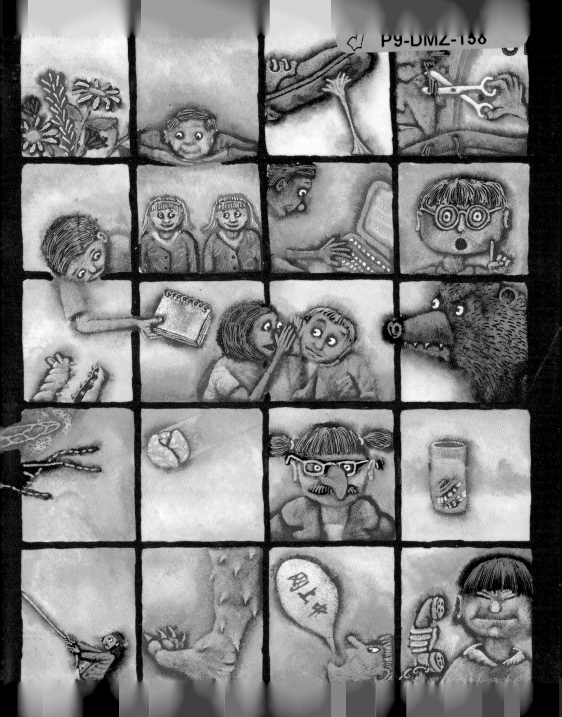

Dial Books for Young Readers

New York

Never Eat ANYTHING that MOVES

Good, Bad, and Very Silly Advice from Kids

compiled and illustrated by Robert Bender

Dedicated to all the teachers and students who contributed to this book . . . and for all the little voices not yet heard

Published by Dial Books for Young Readers
A division of Penguin Putnam Inc.
345 Hudson Street
New York, New York 10014

Copyright © 2002 by Robert Bender
All rights reserved
Designed by Kimi Weart
Text set in Triplex Serif Light
Printed in Hong Kong on acid-free paper

10 9 8 7 6 5 4 3 2 1

Library of Congress Cataloging-in-Publication Data
Never eat anything that moves : good, bad, and very silly
advice from kids / compiled and illustrated by Robert Bender.
p. cm.
ISBN 0-8037-2640-6 (hardcover)
1. Children—Quotations—Juvenile literature.
2. Conduct of life—Quotations, maxims, etc.—Juvenile literature.
[1. Quotations. 2. Conduct of life—Quotations, maxims, etc.]
I. Bender, Robert.PN6328.C5 N45 2002
305.23—dc21   2001017472

The art was created using cell-vinyl paint on layers of acetate.

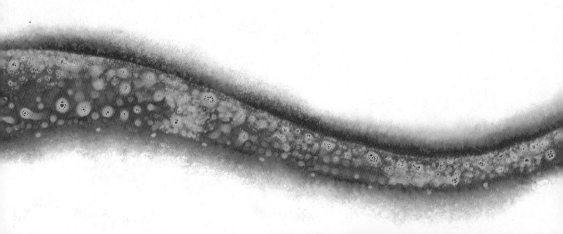

Lima Beans Would Be Illegal was the first book I ever did that featured quotes from real-life kids. Over 100 children told me what they thought a perfect world might be like. But when I finished the book, I still felt that I had only scratched the surface. Kids had so much to say! I wanted to give them another opportunity to speak out and be heard. By choosing the theme of advice, I thought I could learn a lot of interesting stuff.

First I went to the library and got a huge book that listed elementary and middle schools around the country. Then I photocopied *lots* of pages. I visited schools near where I live and made phone calls to those farther away. The question most people asked was: "What's this going to cost?" The answer: Nothing (maybe some stamps). Dozens of teachers helped me by asking their students: "What's the best, worst, or silliest advice you ever gave or got?" Thousands of kids had answers!

I found out that kids care a lot about other people, themselves, and this planet. They are imaginative and wise, funny and weird, and have great sensitivity. Who but a kid would know about how to deal with a monster under the bed, or when *not* to give your dad a free haircut?

My thanks to all the students and teachers who participated in this book. And here's my advice: Listen to kids—they know what they're talking about!

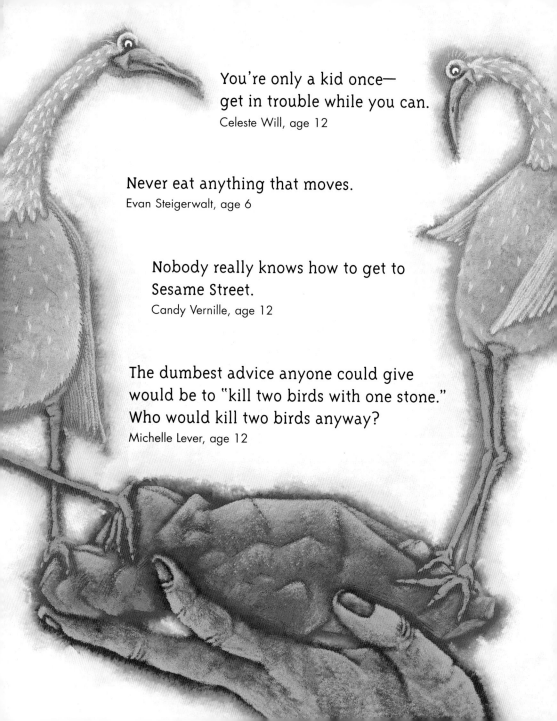

You're only a kid once—
get in trouble while you can.
Celeste Will, age 12

Never eat anything that moves.
Evan Steigerwalt, age 6

Nobody really knows how to get to
Sesame Street.
Candy Vernille, age 12

The dumbest advice anyone could give
would be to "kill two birds with one stone."
Who would kill two birds anyway?
Michelle Lever, age 12

Save a cow. Eat a vegetarian.
David Forney, age 13

My head has learned a softball
doesn't live up to its name.
Danielle Stump, age 11

Don't shave your name on your head,
because they're still going to ask:
"What's your name?"
Ferhat Turkdal, age 4

Never stand in front of a swing
if the person on it has big feet.
Russell Voigt, age 9

Never let your dad set a
mousetrap near the shower.
Del Champion, age 9

If you hide a magazine under your bed,
don't let your mom clean your room.
Shawn Gowin, age 12

I wish that someone had told me that
my brothers would like to wear makeup.
Marian Yoder, age 9 1/2

Before you use the excuse "My dog ate my
homework," make sure you have a dog.
Mariel Solomon, age 10

There is no passageway to the center of the earth, and if there were, your brains would blow up because of the heat.

John Marchello, age 9

Never swallow a firefly, or you might get electrocuted.

Evamarie Bello, age 10

If you cry a lot, you won't pee as much.

Allison Scott, age 8

Don't stick a Tic Tac up your nose (it burns).

Felicia Singleton, age 12

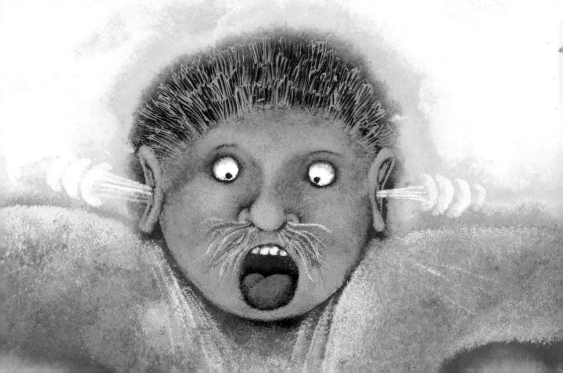

Be the kind of person that
you would like to know.
Steven Crosson, age 12

Try to be the kind of person
your dog thinks you are.
John Allen Fetterman, age 10

You're unique and special,
just like everybody else.
Miranda Skye Gipe, age 10

A dog can be a woman's
best friend too.
Liz Deptula, age 11

The best advice I ever got was
that I was the smartest and
prettiest girl—which I really am!
Latasha M. Smith, age 10

Don't put a bee on a leash.
Jasmine DeGroat, age 7 1/2

Don't move, it won't sting you.
Caleb Whitman, age 11

Never stand behind a cow when its tail is up.
Mary Schnure, age 6

Never milk a cow without an udder.
Aysha Ashley Albright, age 8

Never tell someone "Sticks and stones may break my bones, but words will never hurt me" when that someone is holding a large dictionary.
Alyssa Eichen, age 12

Sticks and stones have never broke my bones, but words have always hurt me.
Stephanie Shattuck, age 11

When your parents fight, don't blame it on yourself.
Nequila Truesell, age 10

Worst advice:
1) He'll grow out of it!
2) This won't hurt a bit!
Laura Rinehimer, age 10

Never try to dress your cat.
Jill Spotts, age 10

Make sure the fish
is dead before you
flush it.
Kelley Stahl, age 12

Hornets chase you a long
distance after you throw
a brick at their nest.
Wesley Cromley, age 12

If you find a mouse and you put it in
your pocket, take the mouse out before
you put your clothes in the washer.
Jessica Chipman, age 9

Never hide your food under the kitchen chair cover.
Bryce Lewis, age 7

Life's too short, eat dessert first.
Jesica Jane Spinks, age 12

Eat the best food last so it will wash away the bad taste of the vegetables.
Tim Fletcher, age 10

Don't lick the beaters while they're on.
Abigial Francart, age 11

If you have broccoli on your plate, when your mom looks away, put it on her plate.
Chase Monborne, age 8

Never eat beans before you to go church.
Danny Adomiak, age 11

Once a waitress gave us fortune cookies. Mine said: "A loved one will perish." I didn't believe it, but one week later my cat got ran over.
Timothy Mark Winters II, age 11

Never leave cookie dough with a three-year-old. They put in "secret" ingredients.
Kirsten Blazic, age 12

Use Brussels sprouts for golf balls.
Matt Fleming, age 12

Bad advice: Always look both ways
before crossing the street, unless
there's an ice cream truck!
Alexis Ham, age 9

Toy army men don't like the oven.
Kelly Evans, age 11

I was outside playing catch.
My dad told me to keep my
eye on the ball. *Wack!* the ball
hit me straight in the eye.
Mario Machado, age 10

Never let your older brother convince you that people *want* you to pee on their house.
Kristan Saloky, age 13

Be one with the basketball.
Rachel May Herron, age 10

Believe me, the dishwasher is not a good place to hide the cookies.
Onyi Nwachukwu, age 12

Don't cross the monkey bars without underwear.
Emily Weatherston, age 6

It's okay to have mean feelings,
but don't be mean to others.
Taylor Beyrent, age 9

Sometimes your best weapon is not
always the one you need to use.
Anna Holland, age 11

If you don't want nobody
to pick on you, just hang
out with me.
Brittany Faulkner, age 8

Just because people
look nice doesn't
mean they are.
Paige English, age 11

I wish someone would
have warned me about
girls when I was young.
David Ruiz, age 10

You know the saying "Take the bull
by the horns"—bad idea.
Josh Blaylock, age 10

Try things that I'm afraid of.
Maria Aguiar, age 12

Never eat chicken at a fancy party.
It could be squid.
Erica Tonia, age 8

Pull my finger.
Daniel Nielsen, age 12

I never judge a book by its cover.
(Half of my books don't have covers.)
Jackie Prebola, age 12

Never imitate an angry teacher.
Shawn Gowin, age 12

I don't know why we have
to go to second grade, we
already know enough.
Cristen Hardin, age 6

I wish my teacher would have
told me about our C.A.T. tests
so I could have failed and
stayed in third grade with
my teacher Miss Pearson.
Gretchen Mey, age 8

Boys are thieves—either they steal your heart
or they take your school supplies.
Julia Berry, age 11

When I was four, my sister told me: "If you want to be a big girl, you have to put your whole butt on the toilet." I tried and I fell in.
Fallon McAnany, age 11

Always look before you zip.
Michael Mazeika, age 13

The silliest thing my friend told me was to hold my pee forever. It didn't work!!!!!!!!!!!!
Ian Hicks, age 9

Keep the lid down on the toilet at night so your little brother doesn't drink out of it.
Morgan Drey, age 7

If you get your brother in trouble, don't smile at him. You're asking for a beating.

Aaron Geiger, age 12

Never live in one house with one bathroom and three sisters.

Katelynn Buccarelli, age 10

If you want to kiss your brother, wait until he is sleeping.

Michaela Marciano, age 7

When my brother had spinal meningitis, I told him: "If you die, your CDs are safe with me."

Mathew Martinez, age 13

A brother is a very precious gift. Spend the most time you can with him. You may lose him one day, like I did.

Gentri Billotte, age 11

If you mix milk with lemon juice, you get something even worse than my sister.
Ezra Margolin, age 8

Do not put your baby sister in the yard sale just because she cries a lot.
Megan Richards, age 8

Your big brothers or sisters will be nice to you or help you . . . someday!
Dylan Robertson, age 9 1/2

Never get in the way of my brother with his six or seven sharp teeth.
Tyler Dunlap, age 10

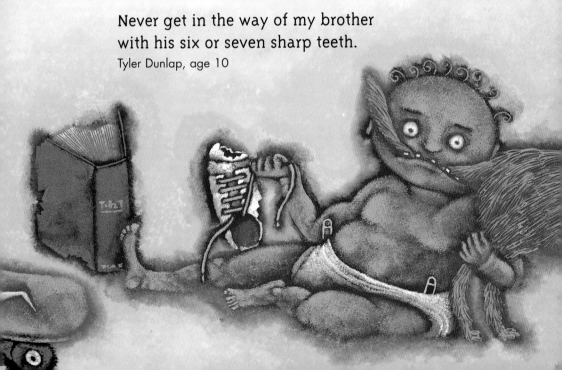

Don't go in the bathroom after Dad's been there!

Julia Moyer, age 6

When your dad says "When I was a boy . . ."
prepare to be bored!

Elaina DeSantis, age 9

I had a soccer tournament and I was *soooo* nervous,
my knees were shaking. My dad said to me, "Just
have fun." I scored two goals in the first game!

Julia Pervola, age 11

Never smell
your dad's feet.

Stephanie Sterner, age 7

When your mom says "Am I speaking Chinese?"
don't say yes.

Angela Eyer, age 9

My mother told me to break a leg
at competition and I really did.

Kristen Marie Blight, age 9

Throw things in the attic when your
mom says clean your room.

Gabe Barrile, age 9

My mom told me when I was really sick,
not to give up . . . to keep fighting. So I did,
and I'm alive and healthy!

Tabitha Watts, age 12

My uncle gives me good advice like staying out of trouble and not doing drugs. One day my gram found him lying on the street because he'd had an O.D.

Drew Parker, age 12

The best advice I gave a friend was to forgive herself for all the bad stuff that she used to do. She took my advice and now she doesn't smoke, drink, threaten people, or think about killing herself.

Tabitha Watts, age 12

I wish somebody told me I was getting a new dad.

Nick Coltharp, age 6

Be a good listener.

O'Neill Petrone, age 6

Dumbest advice: My father told me
to stand on my head, balancing
one cup of water on both feet,
in my underwear, saying
"Hiccups be gone!" three times.

Jareth Tyson, age 12

My mom always says the stupidest
thing—"Keep your underwear clean,
or the cockroaches will come!"

Carl Woods, age 10

My dad gave me advice to
"not smoke," but I caught
him burnt-handed.

Caitlyn Davis, age 9

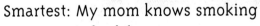

Smartest: My mom knows smoking
is bad for you.
Dumbest: She does it anyway.

Anthony Marino, age 9

Beans aren't fruit! You can't trust
grown-ups with anything.

Ethan Kotkin, age 10

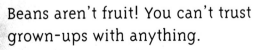

Never go swimming at Reptile Land.

Matthew Hartsock, age 10

If you watch *The Brady Bunch*, don't do what they do when they get in trouble, because it will never work in real life.

Cory Kaufman, age 11

Your worst may be someone else's best.

Lauren Mesko, age 11

Almost anything is easier to get into than out of.

John Duckworth, age 8

Nothing is impossible, it's just difficult.

Christopher Decker, age 10 1/2

Spraying your hair with milk and then drying it
doesn't dye your hair blonde.

Vicky McGowan, age 11

Never slide to first base on concrete.

Tyler Walstrom, age 10

Mud only *looks* like chocolate.

Zach Rhoads, age 7

Never pull a cat's tail or
the other end will bite you.

Brigham Shipley, age 10

Don't try to pull a snake's tail.
A snake is totally tail.

Thomas McIntyre Schultz, age 9

Never eat a frog, or you will get a frog in your throat.

Mengsong Li, age 8

Never brush your dog's teeth
with your dad's toothbrush.

Lizclaire Tamam, age 8

Never eat a magnet when you have braces.

Karl Stengel, age 9

Look in the water glass before you drink.
You might find your grandmother's dentures.

Morgan Georgeff, age 10

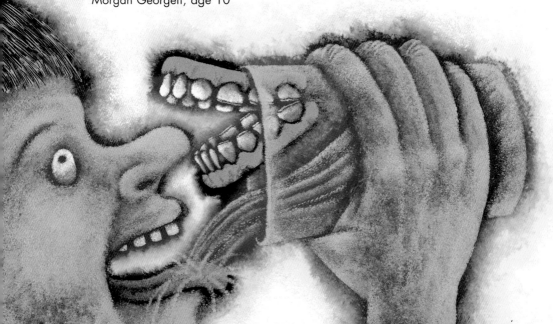

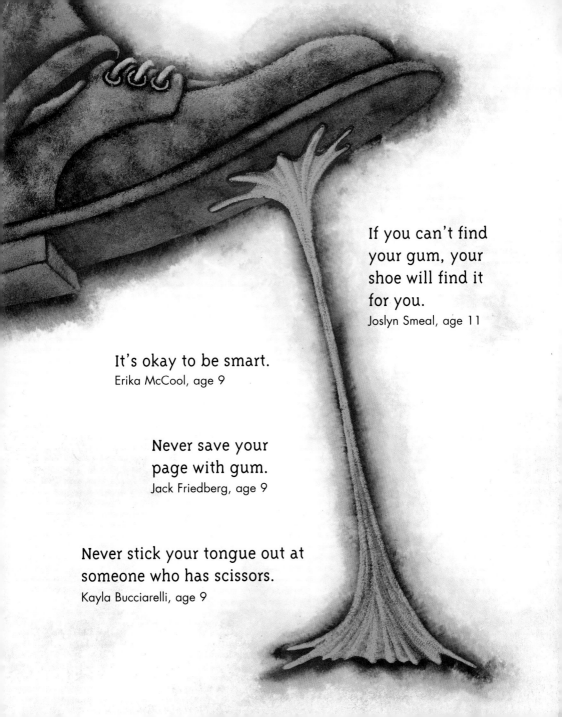

If you can't find
your gum, your
shoe will find it
for you.
Joslyn Smeal, age 11

It's okay to be smart.
Erika McCool, age 9

Never save your
page with gum.
Jack Friedberg, age 9

Never stick your tongue out at
someone who has scissors.
Kayla Bucciarelli, age 9

Never let your boyfriend meet your twin sister.
Christina Englert, age 11

Don't get a girlfriend, it's too mushy.
Eric Werkmeister, age 8

When a guy says he likes you, make sure you know exactly what "like" means before you get really excited.
Kristin Landua, age 13

Don't be mean to ugly girls, because they might have cute friends.
Bobby Petit, age 12

When you find a guy you like, be yourself,
don't be someone you're not, it will never work.
Stephanie Marple, age 12

I wish someone had told me
that boys get more immature
as they get older.
Alexis Reynolds, age 12

Worst advice: If you give
me your money, I'll be
your friend.
Allegra Puls, age 8

One best friend is worth
one hundred lukewarm ones.
Joseph Hyde, age 10

When a bear is chasing you, you don't
have to be the fastest, just faster than
the slowest person with you.

Laura Rinehimer, age 10

You can't get beauty sleep
on an ugly bed.

Tiffany Aungst, age 11

Never think a safety pin is safe.

Maren Bennett, age 8 1/2

Never leave a cat alone at the computer,
it will eat the mouse.

Tonya Worthy, age 9

Smile real big, nod your head a lot, don't say anything dumb, and act like you know what they're talking about.

Sylvia Ann Lee, age 11

The worst advice I ever gave was when my brother asked me if B comes before A. I told him yes, but I wasn't paying attention. When he sang his BACs, it sounded awful.

Desi Casada, age 8

I wish someone warned me that I had misst neighbor on my spelling test.

Lynda Wise, age 8 1/2

Never ask a large woman if she's pregnant.

Chris Perez, age 11

If you play soccer and score a goal, and the other team begins to clap, you might want to score at the other goalie.

Amie Murphy, age 11

Never pee in the pool. This is to keep swimming pools pee-free across America.

Megan Corey, age 12

The dumbest advice I ever got was when my grandma was saying: "You don't have to move, I can see right through you because your middle name is Chrystal."

Ilana Herzberg, age 8

If you think there's a monster under your bed, put your little sister under and listen for a crunch.

Kristen Smith, age 10

Never show an interest in a certain cartoon in front of relatives, or you'll get that cartoon's hats, key chains, sheets, etc., forever.

Ashley Riggs, age 12

When your mom says, "Come here, I got a secret," don't listen—the secret is a big kiss.

Matthew Herb, age 10

You're not in school to make friends. That is what detention is for.

Adriano Apostolico, age 12

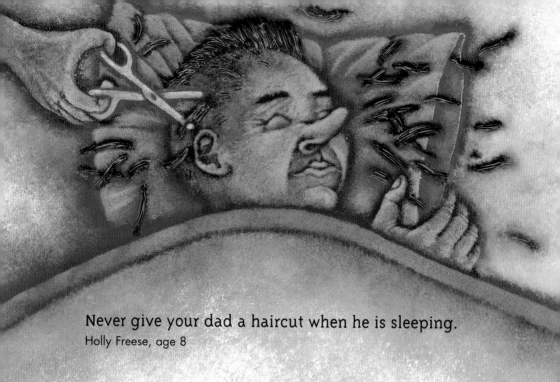

Never give your dad a haircut when he is sleeping.
Holly Freese, age 8

If you get a bad grade on a test, tell
your mom when she's on the phone.
Nicole Murphy, age 11

If your mom says no, ask your dad
while he's watching TV.
Jonathan Sherer, age 7

Wait until after supper to tell your mom
you broke something expensive. Remember:
Always be honest, just not right away!
Kelsey Everett, age 11

My mom always tells me to never get in a stranger's car.
They will not give me back to my mom.

Bryanna Stoddard, age 7

Never pick your nose
when your mom slams
on the brakes.

Lacey Shaffer, age 10

My mom warns me
about *everything*.
Some things I don't
want to know.

Danielle Shirtino, age 11

Be nice to your mom today.

Cameron Rivera, age 8

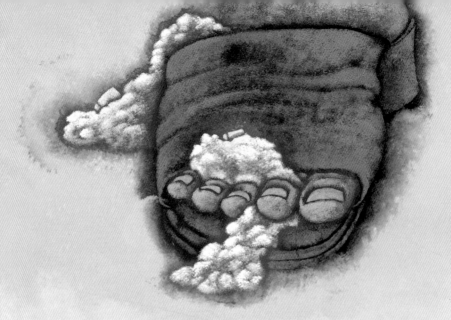

The best advice I ever gave was when I told my brother never never *ever* make mashed potatoes in Mom's favorite shoes.

Megan King, age 9

Never call your parents fat, even if they are fat.

Margaux Labaudinière, age 9 1/2

Old people aren't as old as you think.

Joshua Reese, age 10

Don't take a deep breath when you walk past a cemetery, because the spirits will get inside you.

Zachary Arch, age 7

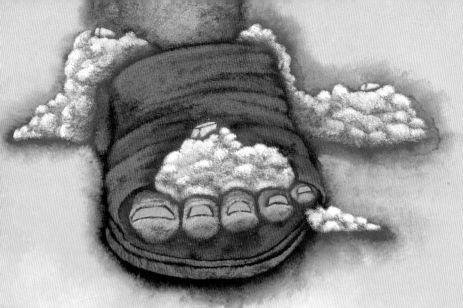

When you get mad, don't let your pain stay
inside, you might break down.

Brittney Robinson, age 11

When I was twelve years old, my boyfriend died. After his
death I became very depressed. I started to think about
death. A boy I know told me that life is a test. It may be
hard, but you can win. Well, here I am, back on my feet,
ready to live and ready to go to high school and college.

Carla Jean Manion, age 14

Tell people that you love them.

Erica Liguori, age 6

If someone in your family dies, don't
let someone tell you to get over it.

Danielle Brethel, age 9

Worst advice: Close your eyes
when you put on your makeup.

Stefanie Shellhamer, age 8

Never kiss your brother
in public unless you have
a good disguise.

Lauren Szewczyk, age 8

If you're stuck in a room
with a locked door and a
piano, use the piano key
to open the door.

Noel Ruggiero, age 8

To sing louder, open your
mouth and pretend there's
an Oreo in it.

Dianna Vo, age 11

Get messy.

Billy Kane, age 11

It's good to be young, because you will last longer.

Cara Iglody, age 7

Don't forget to have fun when you grow up.
We're all kids at heart.

Robert Bender, age 38